Rural
America

The Essential Book of
Rural
America

*Down-to-Earth Buildings
by David Larkin*

*Photographs by
Michael Freeman and Paul Rocheleau*

Universe

First published in the United States of America in 1996
by UNIVERSE PUBLISHING
A Division of Rizzoli International Publications, Inc.
300 Park Avenue South
New York, NY 10010

96 97 98 99 / 10 9 8 7 6 5 4 3 2 1

Printed in Singapore

Library of Congress Catalog Card Number: 96-060689

Half title: Steps at Alford Town Hall, Massachusetts
Frontispiece: Farm buildings in the hills of Virginia

Design Production: Meredith Miller

The Boys' Shop (left, 1850) and the Spin House (right, 1816)
at the Shaker village in Sabbathday Lake, Maine, are evidence of the great
simplicity of Shaker architecture and the sensitivity with which
Shaker buildings were placed on the land.

THE MOST STRIKING quality of rural American buildings is their great simplicity, a simplicity that is apparent throughout the country. It is amazing that settlers from all over Europe and beyond, with their diverse mixture of languages, cultures, and personalities, instilled in their buildings such a pattern of simple, clean lines, devoid of most affectations. These Americans created a harmony of shapes, materials, and function that did not need ornamentation to be complete.

Beneath this simplicity are often clues to an area's history—where settlers came from, what they found in the New World, and what they did once they arrived. Often, rural buildings are not a lot more than a pitched roof. But the angle and size of the roof, the shape of the door and window frames, and the way lumber was cut, among other details, can hint at settlers' roots. The best examples are structures built by settlers who combined materials from their new plots of land with the building traditions of their cultural background. This practice continued through most of the nineteenth century, although structures gradually took on aspects of other building traditions, mixing elements to create a distinct American identity. Only when the railroads were completed and factory-made decorative woodwork and standardized building plans became accessible did Americans begin to move away from these traditions.

A visitor to the North American countryside will immediately notice that rural buildings are spaced confidently apart—they only rarely huddle together. Unlike in Europe, American homes do not sit back from the road in their own exclusive territory. Fences and walls, when seen, are for keeping animals in or out, and trees are for creating shade or windbreak rather than privacy. Mills and churches sit proudly on the road, and farm buildings were often built on both sides of a road, in order to increase accessibility.

Indeed, roads defined the rural American landscape from the outset. One has to travel along the main road out of an American city for many miles to find open country and the "real" rural America. But it is on this road where the historic buildings are, not tucked away down an obscure lane. That came later.

Most of the buildings in this book stand as evidence of how the working lands around them have changed. This evidence is sharply defined where historic buildings have been restored, dimmer in examples like marooned barns in fields of encroaching brush, and dimmer still when the shapes of stone walls and foundations are barely discernible within the returning forests, while the red tags of developers festoon the young tree trunks. The buildings that form the rural past are lessons, examples of what our predecessors did right. What are they trying to teach us? The virtues of simplicity, of course, and of building and living in agreement with one's beliefs and family traditions, the surrounding land, and available resources. A settler could rarely build beyond his means.

These lessons have not changed much over the past two-and-a-half centuries, but they may be more urgent today. The resources of our land, materials, and most important, knowledge, are being stretched thinner, and the built environment has suffered. But with careful attention to our past—whether through preservation, restoration, or simply respect—the simplicity, integrity, and honesty of these rural American buildings can survive.

Francis Choate, the son of a prosperous landowner, built this central-chimney house in 1725 on Hog's Island, near Ipswich, Massachusetts. The Choates came from East Anglia, in eastern England, where the landscape greatly resembles this one in what was once the Massachusetts Bay Colony. The architecture of the Choate House is much like the homes they left behind—save for the incorporation, after the first few years of harsh New England winters, of a great chimney, centrally placed so fireplaces could face into every room.

The small size of this schoolhouse in coastal
Maine reflects the true nature of rural America
in the last century. Land was plentiful for
eighteenth- and nineteenth-century settlers,
and the population in the countryside was
sparse and spread out. While the settlers'
ancestors had clustered together in European
towns, communities here were formed less
readily. Children from miles around came
to the schoolhouse and their parents had
to journey some distance to churches
and markets.

Massive stones compose the walls and entrance
to a cattle pound in Waldoboro, Maine. The
pound was built and used by the town, rather
than individual farmers. Cattle that had
wandered away from their owner's land or
were held in town for other reasons were
penned up here, waiting to be retrieved.

Frances and Rebecca Nurse lived in this large salt-box house in Danvers, Massachusetts, in the late seventeenth century. The shape of salt-box houses (the term derives from the salt storage boxes of the period) is the result of adding a lean-to on the back of a traditionally shaped building and extending the roof line over it. These simple modifications have a great effect, creating a new type of home with a pleasing asymmetry.

To the right of the house is a well sweep, a stripped tree used as a lever to raise and lower the well's pail.

When the Joseph Webb House in Weathersfield,
Connecticut, built in 1752, underwent restoration,
scientific analysis of the house's paint revealed the
original red, blue, yellow, and green hues, which were
matched when the restored house was painted.
Many clapboard houses were not painted at all in the
eighteenth century; the bright exterior and shutter
combinations here must have been a particularly bold
statement in the colonial landscape.

Towns in New England often adopted the place names
of southeastern England, the original home of most
English settlers. Weathersfield also retained the style
of cottages—the practice of clapboarding houses
originated in that region. Indeed, Weathersfield,
Connecticut, corresponds closely to Wethersfield in
Essex, England.

These massive log walls form a corner of
the seventeenth-century Gilman Garrison
House, built in Exeter, New Hampshire, to
protect John Gilman's nearby sawmills
and later used as a private home. Some of
the house's boards retain the marks of the
up-and-down saw in Gilman's mill, and these
logs still have the scars of the hand tools that
shaped them.

The stoutly built garrison lent itself well to
the cosmetic conversion to a private house
once the need for defense subsided. On the
exterior of these thick walls is neatly painted,
white clapboarding; it was only when
interior walls were removed that the scale
of the garrison's construction was known.

The pattern of raised, round bumps on this door at the Parson Capen House in Topsfield, Massachusetts, isn't simply decorative: more than 150 large iron nails fasten an interior layer of thick boards, increasing the strength of the door. Topsfield was located at the periphery of the Massachusetts Bay Colony, where the hostile "wilderness," occupied by sometimes aggressive Indians, began. This door was built to be strong against this real threat.

Rural American fences come in many
shapes and sizes, from whitewashed pickets
to barbed wire. The most enduring and
poetic barriers, though, are stone walls,
symbols of the labor and discipline of
rural life.

The glacial stones that littered the ground
throughout the Northeast and the upper
Midwest were removed by oxen dragging
heavy chains, then moved on sleds to the
edge of a farmer's land. The stones would
then be stacked and arranged as a wall, with
varying degrees of skill, finish, and success.

Clearing the land of its many stones was usually more important than building barriers, and many stone walls are broader than necessary to keep animals in or out. Such broad walls gave farmers a place to put the considerable stone and rubble from their fields. Some walls were actually built as parallel walls of large stones, with a gap between them filled with smaller stones and rubble.

Once built, a stone wall can last more than two centuries and many examples survive from the colonial era. Durability has its price, however; few farm tasks required nearly as much labor as building a stone wall. Only when the land was very fertile could early settlers commit to building full-scale stone walls, although as land became scarcer, more rocky farmland was cleared and more walls were built.

Stone fences extend for untold miles along rural roads, most dating from their region's earliest development. This fence, at Hancock Shaker Village in Massachusetts, evidences the simplicity, sturdiness, and competence that characterize all Shaker building projects. The thousands of squared-off stones that make up the fence were worked with hand tools and serve as reminders of the tremendous labor involved in its construction.

opposite page:
A good stone wall required both labor and skill. Large stone boulders were placed as a kind of foundation, followed by several succeeding layers of varying sized stone. Mortar was rarely used, so considerable effort went into keeping the wall straight and sturdy as it was built. Smaller stones filled in gaps and helped stabilize the larger boulders. The entire arrangement was optimally crowned with long, flat stones that helped protect it from the elements, especially the ice and frost that could easily ruin a wall.

Some eighteenth-century home builders carved grooves into a house's wood facade to mimic cut stone, even painting the grooves white to resemble mortar. (Stone was a much more expensive material.) These carved boards, on the Porter-Phelps-Huntington House in Hadley, Massachusetts, were later covered by clapboarding, concealing but preserving the original facade.

Like many colonial houses, the Peter Wentz House in Worcester, Pennsylvania, has both a winter kitchen and a summer kitchen. The winter kitchen, pictured here, is part of the main house, while the summer kitchen is in an ell at the back of the house. This arrangement kept most of the heat generated by the hearth out of the house during the summer. In the warmer southern states, the summer kitchen was often a completely detached building.

Painted spots in the winter kitchen, and other painted decoration throughout the house, were a playful alternative to wallpaper, which was a luxury at the time. This pattern was applied following traces of the original scheme found during restoration.

preceding pages:
The bright blue and salmon of the dining room
chamber—the bedroom above the dining room—in
the Peter Wentz House are reproductions of the
original colors. The built-in drawers and cupboards
are unusual for a colonial home, although they do
occur elsewhere. (Built-in storage would reach its
pinnacle several decades later in Shaker dwellings.)
A painted pattern decorates the wall at left, below
the chair rail.

An arched opening leads to a breezeway separating
the summer kitchen of the Peter Wentz House
from the main living spaces. The water pump is a
reproduction, but it accurately indicates its original
location, close by and convenient to the kitchen.
The two-tone, painted shutters and door reflect the
Germanic roots of the Wentz family and the region.

opposite page:
Skillfully laid, irregular fieldstone forms the walls of Peter Wentz Jr.'s farmhouse, built in 1758 in Worcester, Pennsylvania. The wood shingle roof overlaps a few inches at its peak—the overlapping side faces the direction most of the area's weather came from, helping to protect the roof against leaks.

A red tile roof covers this bake oven and smokehouse in eastern Pennsylvania. Tile roofs were heavier and more expensive than those of wood shingles, but they were also fireproof and more durable. Red clay tiles like these were used almost exclusively by German settlers, both in this area and elsewhere in America.

opposite page:
The stone barn at Bartram's Garden in Philadelphia, Pennsylvania, is an important early example of the Pennsylvania Barn, a style that became widely used throughout America in the late eighteenth and nineteenth centuries. Built in 1775 by John Bartram Jr., a son of the celebrated botanist, the barn is a unique survivor of pre-Revolutionary Philadelphia's farming area. Although somewhat small, the barn served the younger Bartram well and was an important part of the network of outbuildings on the farm, which also included a seed house, a coach house, stables, and a dovecote, all of which still stand.

The Moravian Single Brothers' Workshop was originally built in 1771 in Salem, North Carolina. Salem was a new town built by the Moravians, members of a Protestant sect who had come to the colony in 1753. The workshop was built in two different styles borrowed from Europe: half-timbered construction filled in with brick, typical of Germany and England, and northern European-style log construction with dovetailed joints at the building's corners. The workshop housed several Moravian enterprises, including a bakery, joinery, hat maker's shop, and weaving facilities, all operated by the single men in the religious community.

American barns were constantly being improved and adapted to local conditions. This stone-end example in Lancaster County, Pennsylvania, has a forebay cantilevered over the livestock entrance on the basement level. The forebay helped shield livestock from inclement weather, allowed hay and feed to be dropped directly from the threshing floor to the animals below, and expanded the floor area of the barn. The design was adopted across a wide area of the country, from Pennsylvania to the Central Plains and north into Ontario.

In addition to the obvious function of protecting the bridge's
wood structure, historian Eric Sloane suggested several other
reasons for adding a roof to a bridge: it kept the roadway dry
and less slippery, it made the bridge more solid, it kept snow
out, and it might have made river crossings less traumatic for
easily spooked livestock. Once covered, a bridge sometimes
gained other functions, serving as a drill hall, a block house,
or a meeting place. This span, in North Bennington, Vermont,
is known as the Henry Bridge.

With the development of the covered bridge in the early nineteenth
century came an explosion of engineering creativity—there were
almost as many ways to build them as there were bridges. Huge twin
arches spanned the waterway in Theodore Burr's design, developed
around 1804 and widely used throughout the country. The arches
were originally intended to strengthen the vertical trusses, but they
were so successful that they supported most of the bridge and the
trusses ended up being the secondary support. This bridge stands
in North Sandwich, New Hampshire.

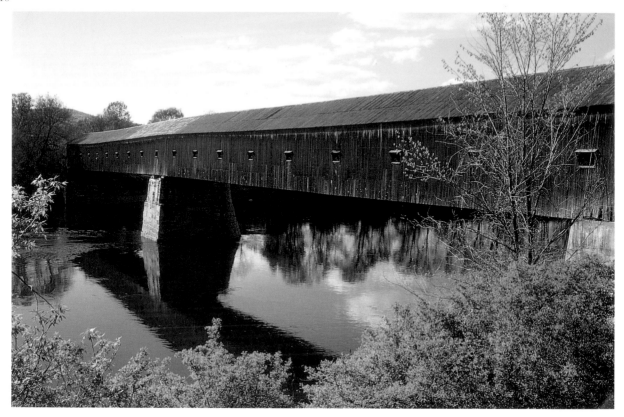

Covered bridges were adapted for communities across the
continent, from Maine to Alabama to Oregon. The form
a bridge took was usually specific to its region: in New
England, the spare lines and minimal decoration associated
with the area's domestic architecture were reflected in its
bridges, including the fine Cornish-Windsor Bridge linking
New Hampshire and Vermont.

The lattice truss, patented by Ithiel Town in 1820 and improved
in the following decades, was a simple and economical way to
support a covered bridge. Construction was easier than with
a double-arched bridge, shorter and cheaper lengths of wood
could be used, and the design did not strictly limit the length
of the bridge. As the many surviving examples prove, Town's
design was a strong and long-lasting one.

This spectacular living room is the main open space of a converted eastern Pennsylvania barn reerected in Southampton, New York. The barn's basic volume and structure were preserved, and the rich textures of the materials create a warm atmosphere and a fine backdrop for the owners' collections of folk art and Arts and Crafts furniture.

Thick vine branches serve as a banister for a corner stairway in the converted barn. The sinuous branches are an interesting counterpoint to the strong, straight lines of the barn's framing and reflect the owners' eclectic tastes.

The intricate and elegant framing under the curved roof of the
Shaker meetinghouse in New Lebanon, New York, allowed the
building's first floor to be completely open, with no support
columns. The largest Shaker house of worship in America, the
meetinghouse hosted Sunday meetings of as many as five hundred
Shakers and one thousand visitors. A curved ladder used for roof
repairs rests on the attic's boardwalk.

The Gothic tie-beam timber roof at St. Luke's Church, near Smithfield, Virginia, allows the church floor to be open and free of support columns. Begun in 1632, St. Luke's is the only original Gothic church in America. It is said to have been erected by shipbuilders; the graceful roof framing resembles the keel-less hull of a large ship.

following page:
Completed by John Drayton in 1742, Drayton Hall, near Charleston, South Carolina, is one of the finest and best preserved Georgian homes in America. Later generations of the Drayton family used the home only occasionally and never added electricity, running water, or central heating, preferring to keep the house close to its original state. The double staircase at Drayton Hall's entrance is made of West Indies mahogany; its hand-carved details and the plasterwork underneath and in the hall beyond are all original.

This wrought-iron rat-tail hinge on a cupboard door in Salem, North Carolina, is common in Moravian furniture. The rat-tail hinge is both elegant and practical, for it allows the door to be removed more easily than a normal hinge would.

A wrought-iron snake and desert mouse form a door latch at San Xavier del Bac, outside Tucson, Arizona.

With its famous bulbous profile, San Francisco Mission Church at Rancho de Taos, New Mexico, is the icon of Spanish colonial architecture. The church's plan was made in the shape of the cross—two vestries stand on either side of the main sanctuary (in the foreground) and the nave, which extends toward the front of the church.

The great notoriety of the rear of the church is probably owed to its traditional placement: the church faces onto a plaza, as most Spanish churches do. However, the main street of Taos does not run through the plaza, it runs to its side, passing by the rear of the church and exposing it to the scrutiny of countless visitors.

Without constant care, the weather can quickly damage adobe buildings beyond repair. Rain water turns exposed adobe bricks back into mud, and winter's freezing and thawing can crack the outer plaster shell.

An arch at San Miguel Arcángel, in San Miguel, California, recalls the architecture and decoration of the Mediterranean. Built between 1816 and 1818, the mission is remarkably well preserved, with most of its painted decoration, as well as the great retablo in the sanctuary, still intact.

La Purísma Concepción Mission, near Lompoc,
California, was rebuilt almost from scratch by the
Civilian Conservation Corps in the 1930s. Young
men, most from southern California and many of
Hispanic background, tried to replicate the mission's
original processes and finishes. They reconstructed
the buildings by hand, making their own adobe
bricks and clay tiles from local materials and
following archeological evidence and the sparse
documentation and ruins that existed. The completed
mission, now maintained as a state park, movingly
re-creates the feel of Spanish California.

Once an outpost of European Christendom, Nuestra Señora de Los Angeles de Porciuncula in Pecos, New Mexico, now stands as a testament to the ravages of time. When the National Park Service acquired this site, a complete renovation was not undertaken: the ruined mission told much more about the history of the Spanish Southwest than a reconstruction could. The Park Service instead stabilized the ruin, so it would stand as it does today, with no further deterioration to its eloquent silhouette.

Thick, plaster-covered walls and massive wood ceiling
beams define the character of adobe interiors. For
architectural and aesthetic reasons, the corners of an
adobe building are not exact angles, and the walls are
not perfectly straight or absolutely vertical. Instead,
they flow in gently varying lines and textures,
softening the feel of the space. The weathered door
and rough plank pine cupboard are reminders of
both the early settlement of the region and its
long-standing building traditions.

Nuestra Señora de la Asunción at Zia Pueblo,
New Mexico, is a wonderful example of the
Southwestern mission. Tall adobe walls with large
buttresses frame the modest building; the curving
walls stand humbly but sturdily under the great
New Mexican sky. Traditional Anasazi cloud motifs,
symbols of the power of the heavens, provided the
model for the shape of the bell tower.

Spanish settlers in the late sixteenth and early seventeenth centuries brought new tools and building techniques to New Mexico, expanding the range of the native adobe architecture. Longer and thicker vigas—heavy ceiling beams of fir or spruce— allowed the Spanish to build wider rooms, which could be extended to almost any length. *Latillas*—small laths or poles— cover the spaces between the vigas, forming the completed ceiling interior and supporting the adobe roof above.

A dramatic ring of granite rocks in New Mexico shapes the structure and feel of this contemporary house. Smoothly contoured, adobe-style walls, the massive boulders, and plenty of natural light create a tranquil balance of elements, an almost perfect combination of the natural and the man-made.

Old and new elements are skillfully combined in this home set amidst huge New Mexican rocks. Vigas radiate from a circular, skylit room with adobe-like walls; thin milled wood slats replace the traditional *latillas*, allowing a modern infrastructure to be installed. The combination of contemporary and ancient creates a home with respect for the most basic elements—wood, rock, plaster, and light—as well as modern conveniences.

In certain places, where cultural influences have met, regional building methods have been combined in distinctive ways. Here, in the village of La Cienaga, New Mexico, the gently sculpted form of an adobe chimney complements and forms a contrast with the building's rough log construction, a form native to northern and western Europe.

opposite page:
The raw, simple materials and styles that defined rural American structures in the eighteenth and nineteenth centuries are just as effective today in creating comfortable and interesting living spaces. Large, stripped logs and mortared fieldstone form the interior walls of this contemporary house in western Massachusetts. The texture and presence of the logs and stone give this house a great deal of interest and integrity, leaving little need for additional decoration.

Many nineteenth-century immigrants moved south from their ports of entry in the Northeast, settling in the southern Piedmont area and west into the Appalachians. These settlers introduced northern European building styles to the South, notably the simple and sturdy log house, taking advantage of the then abundant lumber sources. The white picket fence was used to keep foraging animals out of the vegetable garden and here makes a strong contrast with the raw, unpainted surface of the log buildings.

Set in a giant fir tree in the Northwest, this round treehouse commands a 360-degree view of the surrounding forest. Built by a master treehouse builder, the house is elaborate and large, with nearly two hundred square feet of space inside, but still simple enough not to be out of place in a tree. The house was constructed in sections on the ground, which were then hoisted thirty feet up and assembled atop the sturdy supports and joists. A deck was added later.

This traditionally styled treehouse is firmly anchored twenty feet off the ground in an Oregon white oak. Part of a forty-acre resort in Takilma, Oregon, the treehouse provides gracious, light-filled accommodations for its many visitors. Large clerestory windows offer a wonderful view of the surrounding treetops, and the wide deck serves as a peaceful outdoor vantage point.

Treehouses have a history of at least three hundred years in Western architecture and much longer in the tropics. Although well-weathered, these two treehouses in Eureka, California, date only to the 1970s, when they were built of driftwood and tree limbs. Amid a sea of ranch houses, they are wonderful examples of vernacular architecture and have been a great attraction for the neighborhood's children.

These vacation cottages on Martha's Vineyard, Massachusetts, decked out for a summer celebration, are nicely preserved examples of the "gingerbread" Victorian style, which was adopted for homes both great and small. The cottages also incorporate elements of the Shingle style—namely, the shingle cladding—that was popular on the northeast coast but usually found on large, high-style homes.

Geographic isolation has helped preserve much of the architectural heritage of Key West, Florida, which is especially rich in Victorian-style homes. The J.Y. Porter House demonstrates how easily Victorian decoration was added to existing regional home styles: the classic boxy, two-story southern home with a porch is enlivened with exuberant spindlework balustrades and decorative, half-arch porch supports.

Rapid industrial progress and the completion of the railroad network in the second half of the nineteenth century encouraged the manufacture and use of fancy detailing on homes throughout the country. The level of intricacy previously reserved for homes of the wealthy became widely accessible when standardized (but elaborate) architectural features were first mass-produced and shipped inexpensively to all points. The elaborate balustrades on this house in Key West are typical of factory-produced exterior details.

When American builders adopted balloon framing—building a light frame of two-by-fours rather than heavy timbers—for most of their construction in the mid-nineteenth century, they gained the freedom to build in almost any shape they or their clients desired. Towers, multiple roof lines, bay windows, and elaborate layouts became common in the Victorian era in a great rush toward architectural complexity and creativity. The Richard Peacon House in Key West was built in the shape of an octagon, a style that reached many areas of the country, although only a few thousand examples were built.

Author's note:
All the buildings illustrated in this edition
were photographed by Michael Freeman and
Paul Rocheleau. I would like to thank the owners
and institutions for their generous cooperation.

Michael Freeman:
*Front cover, back cover, 5, 8–9, 14–15, 16, 17, 25,
44–45, 47–right, 49, 51, 52–53, 54–55, 56–57, 58–59,
60–61, 63, 65, 66*

Paul Rocheleau:
*Half title, frontispiece, 10–11, 12–13, 19, 20–21,
22–23, 24, 26–27, 28–29, 30–31, 32, 33, 34–35, 36–37,
38–39, 40–41, 42–43, 46, 47–left, 67, 68–69, 70–71,
72–73, 74–75, 76–77, 78–79, 80*

A detail from Caroline Street in Key West, Florida.